BIRDS
OF NEW ZEALAND
PHOTOGRAPHY BY ROB SUISTED
TEXT BY ALISON DENCH

NEW
HOLLAND

CONTENTS

INTRODUCTION

A fearless fantail dashes around the feet of a hiker. A kea lifts off with a flash of scarlet under its wings. A gannet soars above the waves searching for fish. A long-legged pukeko paddles awkwardly across a grassy field. Late at night, a male kiwi makes a whistling call to his mate. These are the sights and sounds of New Zealand, land of birds.

When, some 85 million years ago, New Zealand drifted away from the supercontinent of Gondwana, it took with it a Noah's ark of plants and animals. These species evolved in isolation into a unique ecosystem with an extraordinary range of birds and virtually no land mammals except for bats.

Without terrestrial predators or competition for food on the ground, the birds evolved quite differently from birds anywhere else. Many came to occupy the ecological niches usually inhabited by mammals. Some, like the kiwi, became too bulky and heavy to fly. Others, such as Haast's eagle, the giant penguin and the moa (all now extinct) grew to enormous size. Parrots, usually tropical birds, adapted to life in temperate forests and cool alpine areas. But this bird paradise could not last forever. With the arrival of humans and their hangers-on – rats, dogs, cats and more – came predation and habitat destruction. Rats and stoats thrived on the birds' eggs and nestlings, the bigger birds were hunted for meat, and forests were cleared for farming – until one-third of the native bird species were wiped out. Settlers also brought foreign birds, many of which became established in New Zealand, and not always with positive results.

A quarter of the species found here today live nowhere else on the planet, and these endemic species are especially vulnerable. Fortunately, New Zealand is a world leader in bird recovery science and thanks to the efforts of the Department of Conservation and volunteer groups such as Forest & Bird, several species on the brink of extinction have been brought back to viable population levels. These organisations have also adopted a number of sanctuaries and cleared them of predators and pests. The result is that in many places around the country the air once again rings with the melodious songs of forest birds, the chattering of parrots, the distinctive calls of wetland birds and the harsh cries of seabirds.

Left: New Zealand's smallest tern is the fairy tern/tara-iti.

FOREST BIRDS

FOREST BIRDS

At the time humans first arrived in New Zealand some 800–900 years ago, about four-fifths of the land was covered in forest, which would have echoed to the song of uncountable native birds. Today, that figure is more like one-fifth. The forest types vary – the North Island has mostly conifers and broadleaf trees, whereas the South Island generally has beech trees – but all remain important habitat for birds. Many bird species are present throughout the country, even if there are often distinct North Island and South Island subspecies that differ in appearance and song dialect.

Left: The bellbird/korimako (or makomako) has a clear and ringing song interrupted by the occasional grunt. It is one of only a few species that sing for most of the year.

Above: A brown kiwi probes the forest floor at night in search of invertebrates and fallen fruit. New Zealand's national bird has lost the ability to fly – but when spooked it can run fast on its sturdy legs.

Above: Loyal to their mates, blue duck/whio are almost always seen in pairs. They live on fast-flowing streams in mountains, forests and grasslands away from human development.

Right: The kaka is a forest parrot with a powerful bill for ripping bark off trees to feed on insect larvae. Pairs nest in spring and summer in dry tree holes. These are social birds that form large, chattering flocks at dawn and dusk.

Below and right: The kakapo is the world's heaviest parrot – and the oddest, too. Despite having big wings it cannot fly, preferring to walk, jump and climb. It is nocturnal. It brays like a donkey and squeals like a pig, and the male utters a deep bass boom to attract his mate. The species is critically endangered, and its tiny population lives only in the protected environment of kakapo sanctuaries.

Left: The kokako, with its rich flute-like call, is a haunting but all too rare presence in New Zealand's forests. A weak flier, it has fallen victim to the introduced possum and stoat and is a threatened species; the South Island subspecies, with its orange wattles, may now be extinct.

Right: The morepork/ruru, New Zealand's only surviving native owl, is common in forested areas of both islands. Both English and Maori names mimic this bird of prey's call, which includes a repeated, monotonous double hoot.

Left: Now scarce in its natural habitat – the native forests of both North and South Islands – the red-crowned parakeet/kakariki has a stronghold in Stewart Island/Rakiura and other offshore islands. This slender and agile parrot is one of six species of parakeet found only in New Zealand.

Right: The New Zealand pigeon has several Maori names including kereru and kukupa. It announces its presence in the forest with a burst of whistling, rhythmical wingbeats as it flies from tree to tree in search of food. The kereru is the only fruit eater big enough to swallow some berries whole, and many trees, including karaka and taraire, are entirely reliant on this bird for seed dispersal.

Above: The rifleman/titipounamu is, at 6–7g in weight, New Zealand's smallest bird. It has almost no tail, and gets around mostly by hopping from branch to branch, clinging on easily with its oversized feet.

Right: With their long thin legs, upright stance and inquisitive nature, New Zealand robins/toutouwai broadly resemble British robins, though they are not closely related. This male South Island robin is distinguished from North Island counterparts by the yellowish tinge of his grey-white breast.

Above left: The fantail/piwakawaka uses its long tail feathers to steer its twisting aerobatics when hunting insects in flight.

Below left: The silvereye or waxeye has a love of fruit that often takes it out of the forests into gardens. Its Maori name, tauhou, means 'stranger'.

Above: The saddleback/tieke, a ground-feeding bird, is very vulnerable and was driven almost to extinction by introduced predators. Today, the only remaining saddleback populations are in mainland and offshore island sanctuaries.

Above: A victim of introduced predators, the stitchbird/hihi was by 1885 extinct everywhere except Little Barrier Island to the north of Auckland. Promising attempts are being made to re-establish mainland populations. While the male (shown here) is boldly coloured, his mate's plumage is a more drab range of browns.

Right: The male South Island tomtit/ngirungiru has a yellow breast, in contrast to its white-breasted North Island cousin, the miromiro. Some Maori believed the tomtit had special sacred status and its appearance was thought to predict good news.

Left and above: The tui is easy to identify by its iridescent dark plumage and bushy white throat tuft. That said, you are more likely to hear its beautifully expressive song of whoops, clucks, chucks and wheezes before the singer itself comes into view. Tui are talented mimics: sometimes they imitate the songs of other birds, and Maori tamed them and taught them to speak.

Left: The flightless weka, inquisitive and bold, is a large brown rail. It is omnivorous and uses its strong bill to take on anything from larvae to rats, as well as tasty or shiny items left lying around by campers and hikers. When a weka gets up speed as it heads for cover, its head-outstretched running style is unmistakable.

Above: The grey warbler/riroriro is a very small forest bird that builds a remarkable pear-shaped hanging nest. It often flits around and hovers among the foliage on the lookout for invertebrates. The song is a delicate and musical trill, which Maori heard as a reminder to plant their crops in spring.

WETLAND BIRDS

WETLAND BIRDS

Most parts of New Zealand get plenty of rain, and that means that there are plenty of swamps, bogs and lakes. But there are not nearly so many as there used to be. Nearly one-third of our native birds rely on wetlands for food and breeding, and many have become extinct as humans have drained their habitat for suburban housing and farmland. Fortunately, there has been a trend recently to restore the once-scorned wetlands, and populations of some of our unique water-loving birds are starting to increase again.

Left: The New Zealand scaup/papango is a small native duck with a classic 'rubber-duck' profile; the male (shown) sports glossy black plumage, while his mate is a duller brown. The bird's enormous webbed feet make it a powerful diver – it can reach depths of 3 m – but are something of a handicap on land, where it is clumsy and slow.

Above: The New Zealand shoveler/kuruwhengi earns its name by sifting seeds and small aquatic creatures through its large scoop-shaped bill as it swims. It is a swift flier with narrow pointed wings.

Above: The black shag/kawau is just as happy fishing in fresh water as it is in the sea, and may be found all over New Zealand. The species has a wide global distribution; in the northern hemisphere it is known as the great cormorant.

Right: The Australasian crested grebe/kamana (or puteketeke) lives on clear freshwater lakes. Before mating, male and female engage in a graceful courtship dance. Eggs are laid on a floating nest.

Left and below: The New Zealand kingfisher/kotare is a wary bird, admired by Maori as an effective sentry. It is also an able hunter, killing larger prey such as fish or lizards by bashing them on rocks.

Right: A mallard touches down on water. This introduced duck feeds by dabbling in the water and upending in traditional duck style. It is very common and is hunted as game.

Above and left: Unusually among ducks, the female paradise shelduck/putangitangi is showier than the male, with her striking white head and chestnut body. This large, almost goose-like bird is found only in New Zealand.

Right: It is unusual to see the fernbird/matata, a secretive bird that tends to stay within the camouflage of dense scrub. Fernbirds are reluctant fliers, and when forced into the air they stay low with their tails held down.

Above: The banded rail/moho-pereru is a shy, rarely seen relative of the weka. This once-widespread native bird is now restricted to Stewart Island/Rakiura and the northernmost parts of the other two main islands.

Right: The natural home of the pukeko (a swamp hen) may be the wetlands, but it often strays onto grasslands, not to mention busy roadways. It carries a heavy body on long legs with massive feet and has a stalking stride, the tail flicking with every step.

Left: The flightless Campbell Island teal is one of the rarest ducks in the world. Very few people have seen this shy, mainly nocturnal bird in the wild. It has been rescued from near extinction with a captive breeding programme.

Right and below: The brown teal/ pateke was once the most common wetland bird species, but now it is endangered. It roosts in flocks during the day and dabbles for food during the evening and night.

Left and below: The royal spoonbill/kotuku-ngutupapa is from the same family as the ibis. It feeds by walking slowly through the water, sweeping its partly open flat bill from side to side. The species is new to New Zealand; it was self-introduced from Australia in the 20th century.

COASTAL AND SEABIRDS

COASTAL AND SEABIRDS

With its long coastline, numerous offshore islands and waters teeming with fish, New Zealand is a paradise for birds that rely on the sea. About one-quarter of the world's seabird species breed here, some in huge colonies on the mainland where they are easy to observe. These seabirds find most or all of their food out at sea, while shorebirds find rich pickings in harbours and estuaries, tugging marine worms, crustaceans and molluscs from the tidal mudflats or scooping up small fish. Between them the birds of the coast and sea show an intriguing range of adaptations to their environment, whether it's a penguin's flipper-like wings, an albatross's long-range flying ability or a stilt's long legs.

Left: Also known as the sea swallow because of its forked tail and agile flight, the white-fronted tern/tara is the most common of New Zealand's terns. These coastal birds form large flocks when fishing.

Above: In New Zealand the fairy tern/tara-iti breeds in exposed sites on just a few sandspits in Northland, making it vulnerable to predators. This very small tern feeds on small fish from nearby estuaries.

Above and right: The world's smallest species of penguin, the blue penguin/korora spends most of its time at sea, even sleeping in the water. Birds come ashore only at night, and only to raise chicks in underground nests or to moult; but when they do, they disturb the peace with loud wailing and screaming. Off the Canterbury coast the local population has a different colouring, with more white on the flipper (above).

Left and above: The yellow-eyed penguin/hoiho is one of the world's rarest penguins. Its main breeding ground is New Zealand's subantarctic islands, but it also nests in some southern parts of the mainland. Hoiho are less social than other penguins, preferring to build their nests some distance from each other, and up to 750 m inland. They spend their days at sea, coming ashore in the late afternoon – the perfect time to view them from the concealment of a hide.

Left: An Australasian gannet/takapu comes in to land. Gannets have a wingspan of some 2 m and make spectacular dives for fish. They breed in large colonies on offshore islands or at one of three mainland colonies: Cape Kidnappers, Muriwai and Farewell Spit.

Above: The Buller's mollymawk is, like all albatrosses, a soaring bird, using prevailing winds at sea to cover great distances with very little effort. These diving birds feed on fish, squid and krill. Breeding pairs, which nest on islands, form a lifelong bond.

Left: The eastern bar-tailed godwit/kuaka breeds in the Arctic, but makes an epic non-stop journey of around 11,000 km to visit New Zealand for the southern summer.

Right: The shore plover/tuturuatu is one of New Zealand's rarest birds. The last strongholds of these lovely but defenceless birds are nature reserves such as the Chatham Islands and Mana Island.

Below: The threatened New Zealand dotterel/tuturiwhatu is a plover with an odd little stop-start run.

Above: The white heron/kotuku is a graceful, sedate and solitary wading bird with beautiful plumage. It is rare in New Zealand, breeding only at Waitangiroto Nature Reserve near Okarito, Westland, in spring and summer.

Right: The pied shag/karuhiruhi is a large aquatic bird that offers a striking silhouette when perched, head held high, on a post or rock. Unlike other shags, it is seldom seen inland.

Above and left: Forty-one of the world's 97 species of petrel breed in the New Zealand region. They spend almost their entire lives at sea, either in flight or sitting on the water. This Cape petrel (above) is taking off, while the black petrel has come to land to breed.

Right: The variable oystercatcher/ torea (or toreapango) varies in colour from black and white to solid black. This rare wading bird lives on shellfish, marine worms and crabs.

Left: The pied stilt/poaka, with its black-and-white colouring and pointed bill, stands out in the company of royal spoonbills.

Above and right: Wrybills/ngutuparore form dense flocks when roosting. They are the only birds in the world with a bill that curves to one side – an adaptation that perhaps helps the bird pluck insects from under stones. The plumage offers almost perfect camouflage against the inland shingle beds where it breeds.

Left and below: The royal albatross, one of the world's largest flying birds, breeds only in New Zealand, although it ranges widely over the southern oceans. Royals do not mate until at least eight years old, but when they do, they pair-bond for life.

Right: The endangered Hutton's shearwater breeds in two colonies high in the Seaward Kaikoura Range. While they are nesting, adult birds fly 20 km to the sea each day to feed on fish and krill.

OPEN COUNTRY BIRDS

OPEN COUNTRY BIRDS

For most of New Zealand's 85 or so million years, there was very little open country and relatively few bird species made it their home. Most of the native birds that do live in the mountains, tussock grasslands, wide riverbeds or shrublands, from the cheeky kea to the timid rock wren, have evolved from forest birds. With the arrival of humans, the open country habitat expanded greatly and newcomers have moved in: species from Australia, such as the welcome swallow, and European songbirds released by homesick British settlers.

These pages: The New Zealand falcon/karearea is a fearsome aerial hunter. It swoops, with a shriek, at speeds up to 200 km/h to snatch birds on the wing. Despite its small size it will take on hares and large birds such as white-faced herons and pheasants, and fearlessly defends its territory against its rival raptor, the Australasian harrier.

Above: The takahe, a large flightless rail, was for 50 years thought to be extinct, but in 1948 a small population was discovered in Fiordland. Some birds have since been moved to predator-free sanctuaries such as Tiritiri Matangi and Kapiti islands.

Right: The rock wren/piwauwau is a very small, rarely seen bird that lives above the treeline in the alpine regions of the South Island. It prefers to hop or run rather than fly, and has a habit of bobbing up and down on its perch.

Above and right: The Australasian harrier/kahu is a common sight as it soars and glides above open country or swamp in search of small prey, from insects to birds and rabbits. These raptors also have a taste for carrion, and passing cars often disturb them as they make a meal of roadkill.

These pages: The bold and very intelligent kea is one of the few parrots that have adapted to living in the mountains. They have a mischievous, playful streak and love engaging with humans, generally at the humans' expense. Just for fun, they slide down tin roofs at night, kick snow onto people's heads, steal shiny objects, rip wiper blades off vehicles and destroy tents and backpacks. Kea feed on plants, invertebrates, small animals and carrion – and have been known to attack sheep to get at their back fat.

Above: The chaffinch was first introduced to New Zealand in the 1860s by European settlers wanting a reminder of Home – but unfortunately these seed lovers soon started eating farmers' crops. Today, they are abundant and often visit urban gardens.

Right: The house sparrow was introduced to control insect pests on crops, but like the chaffinch ended up eating the crops instead. They generally associate with humans, nesting in buildings, roosting in city trees and hanging around food outlets looking for scraps.

Above: Starlings were one of the more successful bird introductions as they eat ticks on cattle and sheep, caterpillars, grasshoppers and grass grubs. However, they also have a taste for orchard fruits and compete with native birds for nectar.

Right: Originally from Australia, the welcome swallow introduced itself to Northland in the 1950s and has since spread through most of the country. In between spells of swirling flight, when it shows off its forked tail, it perches on fences or wires.

Left: Its bright plumage makes the yellowhammer, an introduction from Europe, a stand-out presence as it hops and bobs around New Zealand fields. Its song is often rendered as 'a little bit of bread and no cheese'.

Below: The song thrush is known as a musician of great talent with a feel for melody, tone and rhythm. It is also a good mimic, able to replicate other birdsong that it finds pleasing. Introduced from Europe in the 1860s, it is now abundant everywhere.

First published in 2011 by New Holland Publishers (NZ) Ltd
Auckland • Sydney • London

www.newhollandpublishers.com

5/39 Woodside Ave, Northcote, Auckland 0627, New Zealand
Unit 1, 66 Gibbes Street, Chatswood, NSW 2067, Australia
The Chandlery 50 Westminster Bridge Road, London SE1 7QY, United Kingdom

ISBN: 978 1 86966 333 9

Publishing manager: Christine Thomson
Project editor: Olivia Park
Writer: Alison Dench
Editor: Matt Turner
Design: Trevor Newman
Front Cover Design: Andrew Quinlan
Printer: Times Offset (M) Sdn Bhd

Front cover: New Zealand pigeon/kereru.
Title page: The kea is named for its kee-aa cry.
Contents page: The New Zealand falcon/karearea is most often seen in the high country east of the Southern Alps.
Back cover, from top to bottom: Paradise shelduck/ putangitangi; brown kiwi; fantail/piwakawaka.

Photography credits: Dennis Buurman, p18 above, p63 right; Tui De Roy, p37 right; Don Hadden, p54 left; Peter Langlands, p33 right, p61 right

A catalogue record for this book is available from the National Library of New Zealand.

10 9 8 7 6 5

Keep up with New Holland Publishers on Facebook
www.facebook.com/NewHollandPublishers